The Nature Kid's Guide to
LOONS

DAVID ANDERSON

LP Media Inc. Publishing
Text copyright © 2026 by LP Media Inc.

For information address LP Media Inc. Publishing,
30012 Variolite St NW, Princeton MN 55371
www.lpmedia.org

Publication Data

Loons
The Nature Kid's Guide to Loons — First edition.

Summary: "Learn all about Loons, the Nature Kid Way"
— Provided by publisher.

ISBN: 979-8-89818-214-4

[1. Loons – Non-Fiction] I. Title.

Title: The Nature Kid's Guide to Loons

CONTENTS

LAKE LIFE

Loon legs are set so far back on their body that they cannot walk on land — they can only push themselves along on their belly!

Whoosh! A big loon slides across the lake on its belly.

If you have ever been on a quiet lake at dusk and heard a sound that seemed to echo right out of the wilderness, that was probably a loon. There is no other bird quite like it.

Loons are big, powerful water birds with striking black and white feathers, bright red eyes, and one of the most unforgettable calls in all of nature. They float so low in the water they look like submarines cruising the surface.

Every spring, loons return to the same lakes where they were raised, sometimes flying over a thousand miles to get back home. They are loyal, tough, and full of surprises!

LOON LANDS

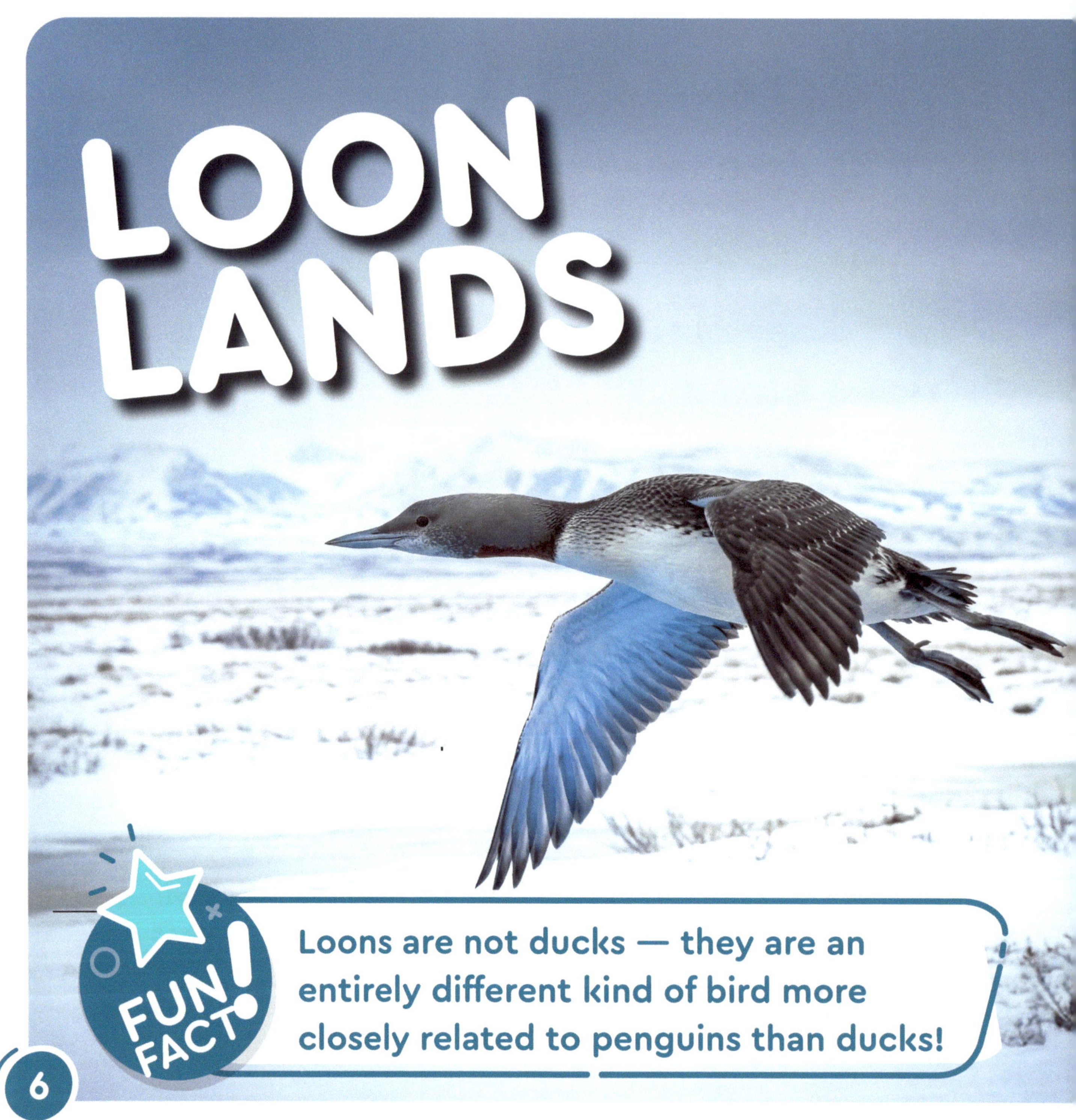

Loons are not ducks — they are an entirely different kind of bird more closely related to penguins than ducks!

Flap, flap! A red-throated loon soars high over the snowy far north.

Most loons live in Canada and the northern United States. Some also live in Alaska. A few types are found in parts of Europe and Asia too.

Red-throated loons have the biggest **range** of all. They live all around the top of the world, near the icy Arctic. You can find them from Norway to Russia to northern Canada.

Common loons are the ones most people know. They nest on lakes across Canada and the northern states. If you live near a lake up north, you might see one gliding by!

SIZE UP

FUN FACT!
There are only five species of
loons in the whole world!

Plop! A big, heavy yellow-billed loon belly-flops onto the water.

Common loons are about the size of a large duck, weighing 8 to 12 pounds. But do not let that fool you — loons are much heavier for their size than most birds.

The yellow-billed loon is the biggest of all five loon species. It can weigh up to 14 pounds and stretch 3 feet from bill to tail. No other loon comes close.

When a loon opens its wings to fly, they spread 4 to 5 feet across. Those wide wings carry them surprisingly fast once they finally get into the air.

BUILT BETTER

Click, click! A loon pops back up to the surface after a deep dive.

A loon's body is built for the water. Its bones are heavy and solid. Most birds have hollow bones, but not loons. Heavy bones help them sink and dive deep.

Loon legs sit far back on the body. This makes them great swimmers but terrible walkers. Big, webbed feet push them fast through the water like paddles.

Loons have sharp, pointed bills. A strong grip keeps slippery fish from getting away. The bill works like a clamp that will not let go.

SUPER SENSES

A loon has a clear extra eyelid that snaps shut underwater — built-in swim goggles!

Peek! A loon spots a tiny fish deep below the surface.

Loons have super sharp eyes. Their eyes can change shape underwater. This lets them see clearly both in air and below the surface.

A loon's eyes are bright red. The red color may help block sunlight and let them see better in deep, dark water. On sunny days, their eyes glow like rubies.

Loons also hear very well. They can hear other loons calling from far away across a big lake. This helps pairs stay in touch even when they cannot see each other.

STAY SAFE

A loon once fought off a bald eagle by stabbing it with its dagger-like bill!

DID YOU KNOW?

Squawk! A loon rises up and beats its wings when a boat gets too close to its nest.

Loons have smart ways to stay safe. If something gets too close, a loon sinks its body low. Only its head peeks up above the water like a periscope.

When a loon feels scared, it may do a splash display. It rises up and beats its wings hard on the water. This makes it look big, strong, and ready to fight.

A loon's dark feathers also help it hide. The black color on top blends in with the dark lake. From above, a loon is very hard to spot.

FISH FEAST

Gulp! A loon tips its head back and swallows a whole fish.

Loons eat mostly fish. They love perch, trout, and minnows. A hungry loon will eat whatever fish it can find in its lake.

Loons also eat other small water animals. They snack on crayfish, snails, and leeches. Sometimes they even munch on water bugs and frogs.

A loon eats a lot each day. One adult can gobble down about two pounds of fish daily. That is like eating 20 fish in a single day!

Loons swallow small stones on purpose — the stones help grind up fish bones in their stomach!

DIVE DEEP

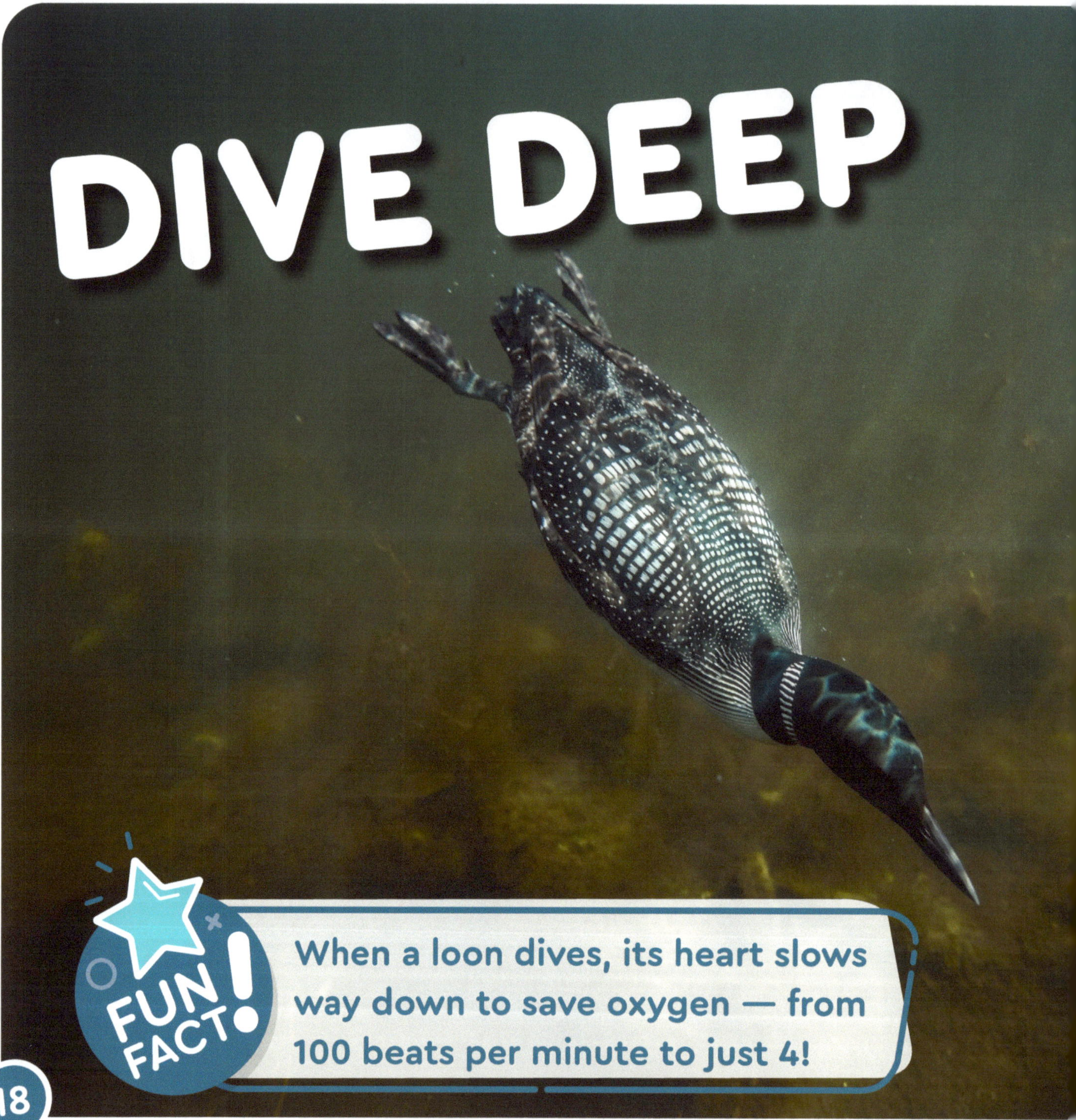

When a loon dives, its heart slows way down to save oxygen — from 100 beats per minute to just 4!

Plunge! A loon tucks its wings and drops below the water.

Loons are amazing divers. They kick off and shoot under the water like torpedoes. Then they chase fish at full speed.

A loon can dive up to 200 feet deep. That is as deep as a 20-story building is tall! It can hold its breath for up to five minutes.

Before a dive, loons push air out of their feathers. This helps them sink fast. Their smooth, sleek body glides through the water with ease.

WATCH OUT
DID YOU KNOW?
Snapping turtles can weigh over 35 pounds — more than three adult loons put together!
20

Screech! A bald eagle swoops low over a nesting loon.

Loons face danger from many animals. Bald eagles hunt them from the sky. An eagle can swoop down and grab a loon right off the water.

On shore, raccoons and foxes sneak up on nests at night. They steal loon eggs when no one is watching. Gulls and crows will also snatch eggs if they get the chance.

Baby loons are at risk too. Big fish and snapping turtles hide below the surface. They can pull small chicks right under the water before parents can react.

QUICK
ESCAPE
22

Whomp! A loon smacks the water with its wings and flies off.

When danger is near, a loon acts fast. It can dive under the water in a flash. It may pop up very far from where it went down, surprising its enemy.

Loons can also fly to get away. But first, they need a running start. They slap the water hard with their feet as they try to lift off.

Red-throated loons have a special skill. They can take off from very small ponds. Most other loons need a big lake to get into the air.

A loon may need to run across the water for a quarter mile just to take off!

SWIM SPEED

DID YOU KNOW?
A loon can fly up to 70 miles per hour, as fast as a car driving on the highway!

Zoom! A loon speeds through the water, chasing after a fish.

Underwater, loons move like rockets. They tuck their wings tight and kick hard with their powerful webbed feet, shooting after fish at full speed. Few animals in any lake can keep up.

On land, loons are a completely different story. Their legs sit so far back on their body that they cannot walk at all. They push along on their belly, which is why they almost never come ashore except to nest.

In the air, loons beat their small wings rapidly and fly mostly in long straight lines.

DAY DRIFT

DID YOU KNOW?
Loons bathe by rolling on their side and splashing wildly with their wings — it looks like a water party!

Flick! A loon shakes water off its feathers in the warm sun.

A loon's day starts early. At first light, it begins to fish. Morning is the best time to catch a meal when the lake is calm.

After eating, loons clean their feathers. They use their bill to spread oil over each one. This is called **preening**. It keeps their feathers waterproof and strong.

Later in the day, loons rest and float. They drift on the calm water with their head tucked back. By evening, they fish one more time before dark.

LOON PAIRS

FUN FACT!
If a stronger loon shows up, it may fight the old one and take over the whole lake!

Coo-oo! Two loons float side by side on a peaceful lake.

Loons mostly live in pairs. One male and one female share a lake all summer. They do not like other loons on their water.

Each pair guards its lake fiercely. If another loon comes too close, they chase it away with loud calls. They act like the lake belongs only to them.

Once nesting is over, things change. Loons join larger groups on big lakes and oceans. It is one of the few times they are not in pairs.

LOVE CALLS

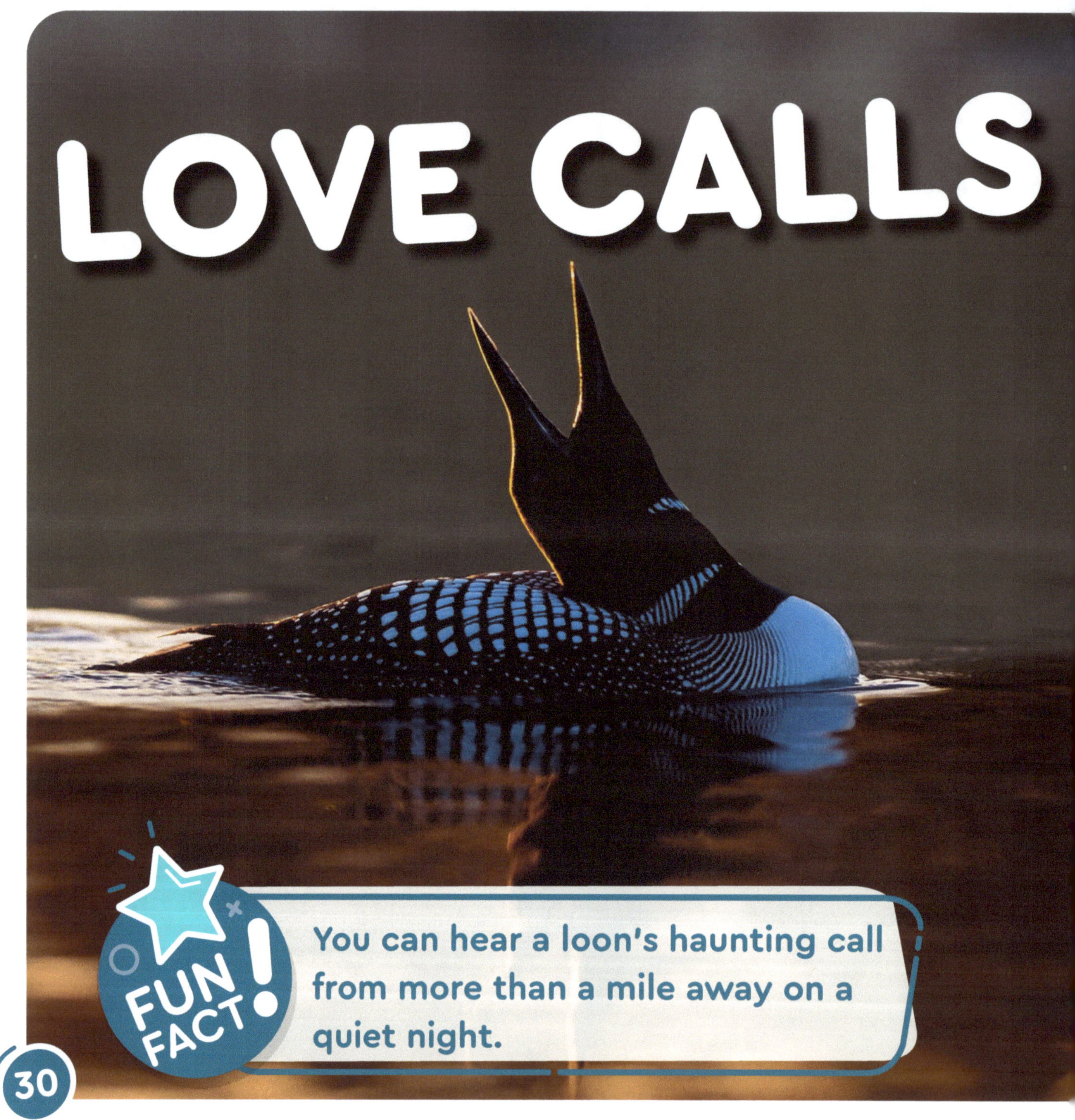

You can hear a loon's haunting call from more than a mile away on a quiet night.

Aaa-oooo! A loon's wild cry rings out across the dark lake.

Loons are known for their amazing calls. No other bird sounds quite like them. People say their cries sound wild, spooky, and beautiful all at once.

The wail is a long, sad cry. Loons use it to find their mate. The **tremolo** sounds like crazy laughter. It means 'Danger!' or 'Stay back!'

The **yodel** is made only by male loons. It is a loud, bold call that tells other loons, 'This is my lake!' Each male has his very own yodel, different from every other loon.

BROWN EGGS

DID YOU KNOW?
Loon chicks cannot fly until they are nearly twelve weeks old — but they can dive for fish at just two weeks!

Crack! A nest of loon eggs is almost ready to hatch.

Loon parents build a nest right at the water's edge. It is made of mud, sticks, and plants. The mother lays one or two big eggs, each about the size of an avocado.

Both parents take turns sitting on the eggs. They keep them warm for about four weeks. The eggs are dark brown with small spots that help them blend in.

When a chick hatches, it is covered in soft, dark **down**. It can swim on its very first day! Within hours, the tiny chick follows its parents into the lake.

PIGGYBACK PALS

34

Hop! A tiny loon chick climbs onto its parent's warm back.

Baby loons ride on their parents' backs. This keeps the chicks warm and safe from big fish below. They tuck in between the wings and hold on tight.

Both the mother and father help raise the chicks. They take turns bringing food all day long. At first, they feed the babies tiny minnows and bugs.

As the chicks grow, they learn to dive on their own. They watch their parents and copy what they do. Soon they are catching fish by themselves, ready to survive on their own.

LASTING LOONS

The yellow-billed loon is one of the rarest birds in North America — only about 16,000 exist in the wild!

Glug! A loon catches a small fish in the rain.

Loons face some big problems from people. Fishing weights made of lead can poison them. If a loon eats even a tiny lead piece by mistake, it can get very sick and die.

Dirty water and oil spills also hurt loons. Boats that zoom too close can scare them off their nests. When wild places are lost, loons lose their homes.

But people are working to help. Many states now ban lead fishing weights near lakes. You can help too by keeping lakes and beaches clean for these amazing birds.

LOOK...
LISTEN
FUN FACT!
The common loon is on the Canadian one-dollar coin — that's why Canadians call it the 'loonie'!
CANADA
2023
DOLLAR

Shh! Sit still by the shore and listen for a loon's call.

You can see loons at many lakes in summer. Look for them in the northern United States and Canada. Bring binoculars if you have them!

The best time to spot a loon is early morning or evening. Sit quiet and still near the shore. Look for a big bird sitting low on the water with a black head.

At night, listen for their wild calls. A loon's cry is one of the most amazing sounds in nature. Once you hear it echoing across a dark lake, you will never forget it.

GLOSSARY

yodel

A loud, bold call male loons use to claim their lake as their own

down

Soft, fluffy feathers that keep baby birds warm

range

The area where a certain animal lives and travels

preening

When a bird cleans its feathers with its bill

tremolo

A loon call that sounds like shaky laughter